For My Little Humming Bird

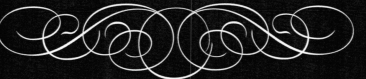

CLAUDIA SUSAN

Print information available on the last page

Rev. date: 05/14/2019

To order additional copies of this book, contact:
Xlibris
1-888-795-4274
www.Xlibris.com
Orders@Xlibris.com

For My Little Humming Bird

CLAUDIA SUSAN

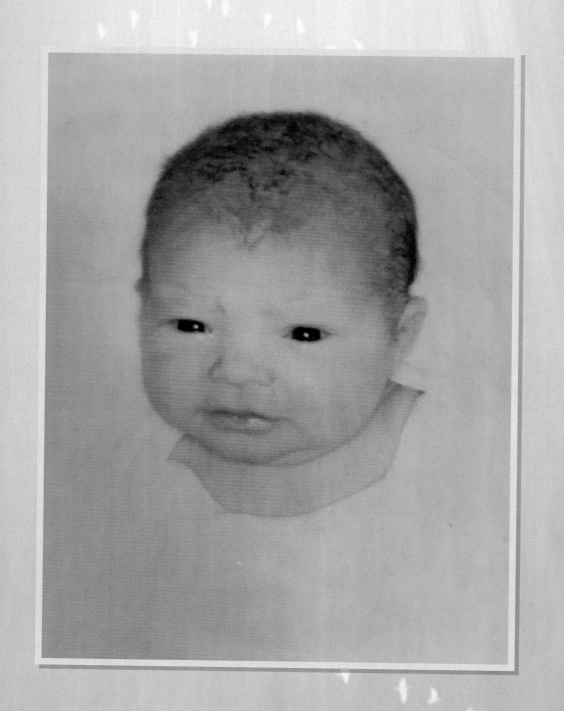

DEDICATION

"For My Little Hummingbird" My Angel in Heaven: Anastacia Lynn Smith and her reasons for living, her four children… Michael, Kassie, MacKenzie and Mason.

INTRODUCTION

This is a work of love for my daughter Anastacia for all who knew her, loved her. For those who didn't know her, a grate loss for you. Her spirit is so present around me as if she guides all that I do. I pray this book honors my girl as I intended to do. You deserved so much in life, but it doesn't always feel as if you had all you could have, especially from me. I will always wonder if you'd still be here if you had a better mother, it will haunt me until my end. But you never complaint, you were always grateful for your children and your life. We always want a do-over, but in this case not possible. Rest in love my beauty, mommy will join you when I'm called home. I love you more than words can say. Xo Mom

TABLE OF CONTENTS

Saint Anastacia

May you be led into paradise
By a circle of Angels
For you are the most
Beautiful Angel, by far.

There will be curly headed cherubs
With fat little cheeks
Gathering together, to sit round your feet

A long satin gown that sparkles in the moonlight
Then like shooting stars
It glistened through the night.

There is a magnificent crown
With flowers inter woven
Colors of yellow and peach.

I wish I could stretch my arm up
And touch you with just one Heavenly reach.

1

For My Girl

A light that shined so brightly
It came from her pure heart,
I do not say that lightly
She was magic from the start.

Her skin was like pure honey,
And her eyes were chocolate brown,
A halo on her head now,
Where there could have been a crown.

Her Grandma called her "sugar Staci",
When she was a tiny babe
That Grandma left this earth too soon,
To see all the sweetness that she made.

Four little miracles she did bear.
Two were brown and two blonde haired.
She loved her babies so, so much,
Everyone could plainly see.

Just look into her eyes,
As she watched her children grow.
What lovely people they.ve become.
She now sees them from above,
While perched on clouds of Heavenly love.

I do believe we'll meet again
My sweet girl and I
Then no more pain and sorrow,
Just a rejoicing will begin.

For the Loss of Love

So, I know that I don't know you well,
But the pain of loss is easy to tell.
The pain in your heart came
out through your eyes.
Pain from loss, has no disguise.
Unfortunately, I have that pain in me.

I don't believe that grief is right or wrong,
So, don't let anyone tell you differently.
There is no need to try and be strong.

Grief is grief and a personal journey,
I promise, in life,
There's always room for learning.

No need to be strong for others around you,
I believe God will love and surround you.
Your loved ones will always be by your side,
While you laugh or while you cry.

It's like having a personal Guardian Angel.
Grief is neither short or long,
Like romantic words in a love song.

So give yourself to those you love,
I promise they'll return it.
And let them embrace your needs,
Self love is not easy,
You have to be willing to learn it.

3

Acceptance

I've said this time and time again,
How do I accept my girl's life
Has come to an end?

She had many hopes and many dreams,
And now all down the drain, it seems.

So, let me try really hard,
To preserve the things I remember.
So many things,
I only long to preserve them all.

You see, my babe was a quiet soul,
So full of life and love.
For her to leave her greatest joys,
This tiny soul was born,
With the sweetest heart I've ever known.

A stranger needing anything
A night in her home,
If that was needed.
The shirt off her back,
And her pants, I might add,
A cheerful smile, and a hug if you're sad.

So, How do I accept my daughter's
Life has come to an end?
I don't, you see,
And that's the point,
And message I'm trying to send.

Her body was sick
But her spirit lives on.
Like the words in a beautiful Love Song.

Acceptance, a choice I'm not willing to make,
A chance with my heart I'm not willing to take.

So, I ask myself,
Time, and time again,
How do I accept my Daughter's life
Has come to an end?

Only her earth suit was taken, you see?
Her beautiful spirit, infinity.................

Broken

There was a little girl
Who's heart was broken....
You would never know it,
Because she was soft spoken.

She did everything she could
To spread her joy and love.
Terrified she'd be found out,
And stand out in a crowd.
It was a daily fear,
God forbid, her voice was too loud.

She never knew how much she was loved.
It breaks my heart
When I allow myself
To admit and to realize,
Our only way to communicate,
Is through the Lord above.

Sweet Baby Girl of Mine

Why did it take you going away,
For me to realize
The things I should say.

The look in your eyes
From time to time
I knew your heart broke,
And so did mine.
All the things that went unsaid;
A joke and a smile instead.

Sweet baby girl of mine
So many things about you,
Made you shine.

Your outer beauty,
Especially your smile.
It lit up the room,
And went on for miles.

Oh just to hold you one more time,
And kiss your cheek,
Would be so sublime.

How grateful and humble,
My heart would feel,
If you believed my LOVE for you was real.

I will still tell the world.
How amazing you were.
My Staci, my daughter,
With a heart so pure.

Like a slow moving river.
My tears will still flow.
My heart will still hurt,
But my mind will still know
Your magnificent spirit

Will continue to glow.

5 Years Gone

It doesn't feel real
When I ask myself,
Where did all the time go?

Is it true sweet girl
In two short days,
You are five years gone?

The time passed so quickly,
Like I've been in a deep sleep,
Five years long.

There's still a cold wind,
Blowing through the middle of my heart.
It won't stop, it's been there from the start.

Your departure was swift,
And felt very cold.
I know you're in a place now
Where you'll never grow old.

Surrounded by cherubs,
With white feathered wings,
And fat rosy cheeks.
In the beginning
Of her departure,
I was angry for weeks
Those weeks turned into months,
And the months turned into years.

Then one day I realized
God had removed the anger and fear.
The grief still remains,
And I want it to stay.
No matter how painful,
I need it today.

But then I realized

But then

8

Hindsight

Hindsight is 20/20,
There are no second chances.
I write these things with a humble heart,
And pray that God can hear me.

The gift of life,
Extended to me,
Her tender spirit I could see.

I envision us sitting side by side,
And you with my hand in yours.
You would assure me, that guilt and shame,
Cannot live in me now or forever more.

What's done is done,
It's time to close,
Then open a new door.

She would say "Mom, you are the one,
That tried to tell me.
The past is gone, the future's not here yet.
Besides, it's time for you to soar.

She has always been my biggest fan,
And I was too blind to see.
The thing I believed
Was that she didn't believe in me.

So, I'll close this poem,
By saying one thing I'm certain of....
Staci Lynn had of magic,
Many people did't see that,
And that is tragic.

But know this about my little girl,
She was such a beautiful addition,
To this often ugly world.

And all she wanted and continues to see.
Is nothing but LOVE,
For you and for me.

Missing You

I don't believe I've ever known
The loneliness feel.
When I remember she is gone
It doesn't even feel real
I miss her so much, my insides feel hollow
When trying to read or pray' barely able to swallow.

Your beautiful smile from ear to ear
Could stop the traffic cold.
Your beauty that shined from within
Will never ever grow old.
The hole I feel in my heart today
Has a fiercely cold wind blowing through it.

Only the Lord can give me the strength
I need to endure it.
So, yes I feel lonely when I focus you are gone
Your body, yes, is no longer here.
But your spirit lives on and on.

January 9th 2017

To my precious Angel
My darling one.
You are the music,
In every song.

There's clearly this,
I know for sure.
When pondering who you were,
Your spirit lifted
Every person in ways so pure.

Not one mean or hateful word,
Came from your loving heart.
Even as a tiny babe,
Your spiritual journey, did start.

In your deep brown eyes,
A message so clearly came.
You touched every single soul the same.
With kindness and love
And a smile behind those eyes....

You drew people in
And they couldn't help but rise.
Your magnetic quality
Was felt by them all
But then, by God,
You had to heed the call.

So, Happy Birthday, my darling Angel,
You are loved and missed by all.

My heart is forever yours,
Until we meet again.
Mama

Heart Pain

My heart literally hearts,
I want my baby back!
So far that's an impossibility,
Life is now and death is such totality.

It is too much to ask,
This I do realize.
I'd give anything for one more look,
Into your soulful brown eyes.

But one thing to look forward to,
Is the day when we'll all
Be together again.

Then sweet girl a rejoicing in heaven,
Family, foe, and especially our friends.
We'd speak to each other,
Without a word,
Communing from heart to heart.

No words need spoken when we go home.
Sometimes, I can hardly wait.
But time will tell,
When that day comes
Arriving at the pearly gates.

Seven Years

Has it really been seven years?
Of begging and pleading
And holding back tears?

I don't want to believe it,
Still to this day.
That you're really gone,
And gone to stay.

I won't see you again,
Until of course I join you,
After you met your end.

My darling, my girl,
I can never express,
The painful tears,
And feelings of distress.

You know many would just love
To silence me
But knowing me, sweet girl
That will never, ever be.

I'll not stop the tears,
Nor sobbing and pleading.
For you to be left,
At your front door, bleeding.

Only you know the truth,
But my instincts are intact.
My heart and head are clear.
And that my dear is a cold hard fact.

Egyptian Proverb

"As long as I have breath in me,
you will never die in my lifetime,
for I will never forget you,
or the things you have taught me.
And I will always speak your name,
Anastacia Lynn Smith.

15

Reunited With Dad

My God, I loved my baby girl,
I only wish she'd known it.
I was a baby myself,
And didn't know how to show it.

There are no words to explain,
Only emptiness and pain.

As you probably know,
Your Dad has passed away.
I feel I am in denial,
Because I'm numb,
And no words to say.

Before he left, I thanked him.
For the miracle he shared with me
Our baby girl, Anastacia Lynn.

And I thank the Lord every day,
For what he chose to say to me.
"We were babies ourselves,
and did the best we could do.
She forgave me a long time ago,
And she also forgave you.

Live your life the best you can,
Be happy and don't be sad,
That's what our girl would want for you.
She'd want it for her Mom and her Dad."

16

Length of Grief

How long do I grieve for you?
Forever and a day......

How dare someone tell me
How long the grief will stay!

I liken it to the ebb & flow,
Just like the ocean's floor,
It rocks itself back and forth,
And breaks on the sandy shore.

And then like the peak of foam and sand,
Like tight strings in a violinists hands,
The part that really amazes me,
Without warning, the powerful sea.

Like rocking on the ocean floor,
And crashing on the sandy shore,
So how long will I grieve for thee?
Forever, sweet girl, eternally........

Escaping Time

Where has all the time escaped?
I stay inside the locked up gate.
I feel as if I am disappearing,
Within my heart and head.
I lay or sit on a pillow clad bed.

While time is ticking away,
All the while wondering to myself
How long will this insanity stay?
I don't know whether I'm coming or going
My resolve is by no means growing.

I need to hold my girl again
And this I know won't happen.
So how do I change the direction I'm going?

I make attempts, but to no avail,
So hold onto the porch
Without the rail.
Step by step, just more fails.

So turn around, turn around,
And go back in. Then tomorrow
We'll try it again.

Desiderata

A poem for a way of life.

Go placidly amid the noise and haste,
And remember what Peace there may be in silence.

As far as possible without surrender,
Be on good terms with all persons

Speak your truth quietly and clearly,
And listen to others,

Even the dull and ignorant,
They too have their story.

A poem written Max Ehcnan
This is written using fair use guidelines

Printed in the United States
By Bookmasters